slow cooking

NEW
HOLLAND

contents

introduction

All foods, as we know, are prone to seasonal change. This is because our food histories and cultural eating practices usually originate from the land, from the simple beginnings of subsistence farming and peasant cookery. There is, however, another kind of food seasonality – different foods come in and out of favour according to the fashions of the time.

What was in fashion 10 years ago is different from what is in vogue today. The fascinating part of the current change in food perceptions is the return of many of the old ways of cooking. Fast food has definitely been put in its place and a return to slow food is very much back in the public's perception of what is both good for you and what is presentable at the table. Within the idea that some of the old ways of cooking are truly worthy and should be enjoyed alongside quick meals, speedy salads and wok-tossed minute meals, there is a strong place for the slow and hearty fireside foods of old.

The slow-cooking pot that bubbled away for hours on the edge of the fireplace made a successful electronic conversion in the late 60s and early 70s and became the 'crockpot'.

Like most fashions, crockpots were heartily embraced and people realised that an appliance that could slow-cook a wet meal automatically (usually without the need for stirring or watching over) was a convenient way to produce wonderful traditional family meals without being tied to the kitchen for the entire day. The crockpot has, however, like many food innovations become identified with the time of its invention and is now seen as old technology. Ask your mum and she probably still has one stashed in the back of her cupboard somewhere or under the preserving equipment gathering dust in the back shed. It will likely be beige or burnt orange in colour with a motif on the side – a testament to the time of its previous popularity.

These cookers have recently had a makeover and with the resurgence of interest in slow food and traditional cooking techniques they are perfectly placed to again be seen with pride bubbling away on the side of the kitchen bench, imparting beautiful aromas to your kitchen while happily cooking away unaided and unsupervised.

Traditional slow-cooked soups, continental casseroles, hearty stews and exotic tagines – the traditional and slow foods from all nations – are back on the food agenda and the poetic and provincial idea of slow cooking inexpensive cuts of meat is seen at some of the finest eateries around the Western world. In short, the slow cooker is back, looking good and ready for service in the modern kitchen.

Once you have started cooking with a slow cooker you will soon realise its convenience and economy. The slow cooker is a low-fuss appliance that is also a low-energy user – once the cooker reaches core temperature the mass of the food helps to retain its own heat and very little extra heat is needed to maintain temperature. Flavours are trapped inside the cooking environment and each component imparts its character and takes on the flavours of what is around it. Good quality stocks, fresh vegetables, citrus rinds and robust flavours such as rosemary and thyme are the winning elements to beautiful old-fashioned cookery.

One of the labour- and time-saving elements of this style of cooking is the fact that you can create the ultimate cooking short cut by cutting up your meats and vegetables and adding them to the one pot (your slow cooker), with the only dishes to wash being your cutting board and knife. The rest is taken care of from cooking to serving, leaving you with only the ceramic insert and the dinner plates for the after-dinner wash-up. There are few simpler and more fundamental ways of cooking.

Getting to know your slow cooker

The various makes of slow cookers respond a little differently to each other so you'll need to gauge cooking time for yourself from the first couple of recipes you try out – if your cooker is particularly large or lower powered then you may need to add a little extra cooking time than the recipe indicates.

For the first few recipes mark down your starting and finishing time so that you quickly get a feel for how your particular slow cooker responds. Keep an eye on your slow cooker in the late stages of cooking to see if it requires any more or less cooking time or a top-up of liquid.

Your slow cooker is exactly that and cannot recover heat losses quickly, so lift the lid only when instructed. If you feel you must remove the lid several times, remember to extend the cooking time a little.

You will learn whether to add extra time by simply looking at your meal in the late stages of cooking.

Due to the unique wraparound heating system, low temperature and long cooking periods, slow cooker temperatures cannot be accurately compared to an oven or a frying pan. So that you can prepare your own favourite recipes in a slow cooker, we have provided a conversion table on page 23.

Cooking settings on most slow cookers are LOW and HIGH. Food will be brought to simmer on all settings. The LOW and HIGH settings determine the time needed to reach a simmer. Avoid sudden temperature changes when using your slow cooker as it will not be able to withstand them. Do not put in frozen or very cold foods if the ceramic bowl has been preheated or is hot to the touch.

The removable ceramic bowl may be used in the oven and is ideal to use when adding a pastry crust to your favourite stews. Be careful not to place the ceramic bowl on the range surface or burners.

Your slow cooker can help you get the best advantage from your freezer.

You can prepare double the usual quantity of a favourite casserole and when cooked, freeze the extra amount. The best way to freeze food for later reheating is to turn it out from the slow cooker after cooking to allow the ceramic insert to cool. Then wash the ceramic insert and coat it with a little oil or butter before returning the cooled food to it. Cover the ceramic insert and freeze until the food is set. Once set,

turn out the block of frozen food and transfer it to a large freezer bag. Then when you return the food to the slow cooker for reheating, it will always fit back in perfectly. Do not use the ceramic bowl for storing food in the freezer indefinitely, and always remember that you cannot return frozen foods to a preheated cooker. When you want a slow-cooked meal without any preparation at all, just place the frozen food into the cooker and heat for 5 to 8 hours. The slow, gentle heating from the cooker will not dry out the meal you are reheating.

You can prepare a recipe the night before in the removable ceramic bowl and store it in the refrigerator so that when you are ready to cook the bowl can be transferred to the slow cooker heating base unit. Just make sure that the base unit has not been preheated. Cook on the desired setting, using a little extra time than given in the recipe.

Most vegetables should be cut into small pieces, or at least quartered, and placed near the sides and bottom of your cooker. Carrots and other dense root vegetables should be peeled and put where they will be covered by liquid.

An unusual characteristic of the slow cooker is that meats generally cook faster than most root vegetables. The heating element of the slow cooker runs around the outer edges of the insert and because of this it is a good idea to arrange vegetables towards that area.

Small food portions can be cooked in the slow cooker, but the times will vary. Because there is no direct heat at the bottom always fill the cooker at least half full to conform to the recommended times. Adjust your recipe volume according to the size of your slow cooker.

Roasts can be cooked on low without adding water, but a small amount of water is recommended because the gravies are especially tasty and it would be a shame to leave them behind.

The more fat or marbling the meat has, the less liquid you will need as the natural fats in the food help to baste and moisten the finished food.

Gravy-making can be done right inside your cooker.

Since the liquid content of meats and vegetables will vary, you may end up with a recipe with too much liquid. The excess can be reduced by removing the cover and setting the cooker on high for about 45 minutes. Most recipes cooked in the slow cooker will be juicier since the slow cooking prevents evaporation.

GRAVY

1. Remove the foods from the pot, leaving the juices.

2. Prepare a smooth paste of about ¼ cup all-purpose flour or cornflour to ¼ cup water.

3. Pour mixture into the liquid in your cooker and stir well.

4. Turn to high and cook, stirring occasionally, until mixture thickens and becomes slightly transparent (approximately 15 to 20 minutes). Then it is ready to serve.

Your slow cooker should never be filled higher than ¾in (2cm) from the top. If it is too full the lid will lift while the food is cooking.

With the high setting, if by chance your dish of food does dry out, do not simply add cold liquid; it is best to boil the kettle and add some extra water, or if you have extra stock, heat it in a small saucepan before adding to the slow cooker.

It is advisable to generally always preheat your slow cooker for 10 to 15 minutes before use. This helps food come up to cooking temperature faster.

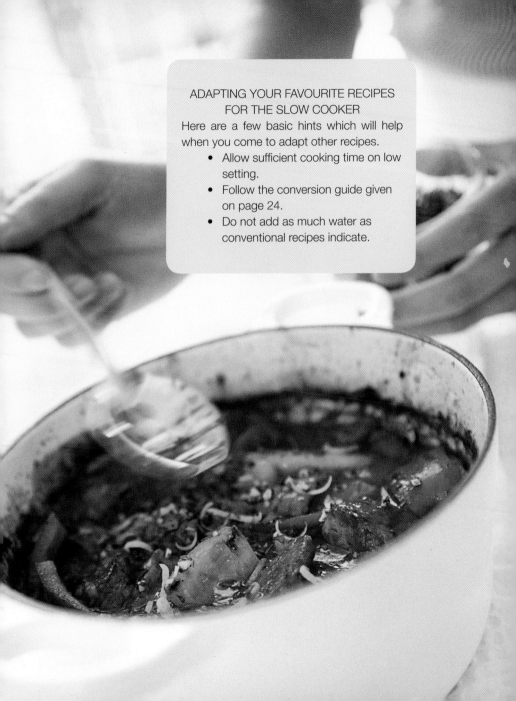

ADAPTING YOUR FAVOURITE RECIPES FOR THE SLOW COOKER

Here are a few basic hints which will help when you come to adapt other recipes.

- Allow sufficient cooking time on low setting.
- Follow the conversion guide given on page 24.
- Do not add as much water as conventional recipes indicate.

Always cook with the cover on. Your slow cooker cooks best if left undisturbed. Lifting the lid can lengthen the cooking time; if you need to stir your dish, do it during the last few hours of cooking time or only when instructed in the recipe.

Generally, 1 to 2 cups of liquid are enough for any recipe unless it contains rice, pasta or other absorbing grains such as polenta, couscous or quinoa. The other exceptions are pot-roast-style dishes where you expect to have liquids at the end and classic Italian styled 'bolito-misto' dishes where you boil and simmer meats and discard the cooking liquid at the end of the cooking process. In the case of the pot roast, any vegetables and the main joint of meat can be lifted out at the end of its cooking time with a slotted spoon and tongs. Then, with the addition of thirsty grains such as those mentioned above, thick and wet rustic-style gruels can be made to form a magnificent base for a truly old-fashioned meal – simply turn the cooker to high, add some grains and cook for 45 minutes with the lid removed (while the main meat is rested and carved).

Slow cooking is one-step cooking – many steps in conventional recipes may be deleted. You can add all ingredients to the slow cooker at one time and cook for approximately 8 hours.

There are three important exceptions: milk, sour cream and fresh cream should be added during the last half hour of cooking.

When cooking with herbs and spices, whole herbs and spices are preferable. When a recipe calls for dried beans, the beans should be soaked overnight, then cooked on high for 2 to 3 hours. Or you can cook them overnight on low with water and 1 small teaspoon of bicarbonate of soda added to speed up the breakdown of the beans. Instead of soaking or cooking overnight, they may also be parboiled first.

When a crisp topping of crumbs or grated cheese is called for, transfer food from the slow cooker to a platter and brown it either with a torch or in the oven. The removable bowls with some models are versatile, as they can be easily put in the oven to achieve the desired topping.

Do not precook seafood or frozen vegetables; just rinse and drain thoroughly before adding to other ingredients. These foods cook quickly, so it is best to add them during the last hour of cooking.

If cooked rice is called for, stir raw rice in with other ingredients. Add 1 cup of extra liquid per cup of raw rice. Use long-grain rice for best results in all-day. cooking

Some foods do not benefit from slow cooking, so do not use any of the following unless the recipe says so:
- Crisp-cooked green vegetables
- Noodles
- Macaroni
- Asian vegetables
- Puddings or sauces made with a foundation of milk or cream

Although these foods are familiar favourites, care must be taken when using them in slow cooker recipes.

You can cook without liquid. For example, fish and sausages can be placed in the cooker, covered, and cooked for 2 to 4 hours, depending on the thickness of the meat. Or, you scrub and dry new potatoes and arrange them in the cooker, cover, and cook for 8 to 10 hours.

GET INVENTIVE

With the guidelines in this introduction you should be able to take any appropriate recipe and convert it to a slow-cooking recipe.

Think outside the square and make the slow cooker work for you. Anything from a hearty porridge with dried fruit slowly cooked overnight to feed a family when it rises for a chilly winter breakfast or preparing a late sweet snack that cooks away as you settle in front of the evening television after the main meal – the applications and variations are virtually unlimited.

COOKING TIME CONVERSION GUIDE

OVEN OR STOVETOP COOKING TIME	SLOW COOKER LOW COOKING TIME	SLOW COOKER HIGH COOKING TIME
15–30 mins	4–6 hrs	1½–2½ hrs
35–45 mins	6–8 hrs	3–4 hrs
50 mins–3 hrs	8–12 hrs	4–6 hrs

This guide applies particularly to casseroles. Most meat and vegetable combinations will require at least 7 hours on low.

All cookers consume approximately the same amount of power. The settings vary according to the make and size and individual style of each cooker, so if you are buying a new cooker, choose wisely and consider your potential end needs.

You can buy cookers with ceramic containers permanently fixed into the outer casings, where the heating elements are placed between the outer casing and the cooking pot. Some of these styles come with detachable power cords so that the entire unit can be taken to the table to serve from.

Another style of cooker has a removable inner ceramic cooking container, which means that only the cooking pot is taken to the table. This style of slow cooker enables food to be easily browned or crisped under the grill for final presentation. In these cookers the heating elements are fitted within the walls of the base unit that the ceramic container fits into.

There are different capacity cookers that vary from 50¾ x 186fl oz (1.5 to 5.5 litres). While the little cookers seem kind of nifty and compact, it is best to get the largest size that you think you can use – once you become familiar with this appliance you will see the benefit of cooking double quantities and large joints of meat. It allows for greater versatility and is an easy way to feed a large amount of guests.

How to clean and care for your slow cooker

- Never submerge the slow cooker cooking unit in water. Remove the ceramic bowl and place the bowl in the dishwasher or wash with hot soapy water as soon as possible after emptying it.
- Do not pour in cold water if the ceramic bowl is hot. When cleaning your slow cooker do not use abrasive cleaning compounds. A cloth, sponge or rubber spatula will usually remove the residue. If necessary, a plastic cleaning pad may be used.
- To remove water spots and other stains, use a non-abrasive cleaner or vinegar.
- The metal liner may be cleaned with a damp cloth or scouring pad, or sprayed lightly with an all-purpose cleaner to maintain.
- The outside of the slow cooker may be cleaned with soft cloth and warm soapy water and wiped dry. Do not use abrasive cleaners on the outside.
- Care should be taken to avoid hitting the ceramic pot with metal spoons or water taps. Do not put frozen or very cold foods in the slow cooker if the unit has been preheated or is hot to the touch.

Safety

When using electrical kitchen appliances, basic safety precautions should always be followed.

- Read all instructions and become thoroughly familiar with your slow cooker.
- Do not touch hot surfaces; always use handles or knobs.
- Caution must be used when moving the slow cooker if it contains hot oil or other hot liquids.
- Close supervision is necessary when the slow cooker is used by or near children.
- Unplug the slow cooker from the power outlet when not in use, before putting on or taking off parts, and before cleaning.
- Use your slow cooker on an even and stable surface.
- Do not place slow cooker units on or near a hot gas or electric burner, or in a heated oven. Only the ceramic inserts should be placed in the oven or under a grill.

soups

Portuguese potato & bean soup

SERVES 6–8

4 cloves garlic, crushed
2 medium onions, diced
2 medium carrots, diced
4 medium desiree potatoes, diced
1 green bell pepper (capsicum), finely
  diced
15oz (425g) canned Roma tomatoes,
  finely diced
½ medium green cabbage, shredded
15oz (425g) canned red kidney
  beans, drained, rinsed
16oz (455g) smoked Polish sausage,
  diced
6½ cups chicken stock
salt and freshly ground black pepper
2 tablespoons chopped fresh parsley
  to garnish

1. Place all the ingredients in a slow cooker on high.
2. Simmer for 4½ hours. Add salt and pepper to taste and serve piping hot, garnished with parsley.

TIP: You'll love the flavours in this satisfying soup. It's incredibly easy to prepare, and since it contains no oil you can make it a regular, guilt-free indulgence.

Porcini mushroom soup

SERVES 6

½oz (15g) dried porcini mushrooms
½ cup boiling water
2 tablespoons olive oil
2 cloves garlic, crushed
1 leek, sliced
6 French shallots, chopped
10oz (285g) white mushrooms,
    thinly sliced
17½oz (500g) forest mushrooms,
    including shiitake, oyster and
    Swiss brown, thinly sliced
2 tablespoons all-purpose (plain)
    flour
4 cups good quality chicken, beef or
    vegetable stock
1 cup double cream
½ bunch fresh flat-leaf parsley,
    chopped
30 fresh basil leaves, shredded
1 tablespoon fresh oregano
salt and freshly ground black pepper
ground nutmeg

1. Add the dried porcini mushrooms to the boiling water and set aside. When the mushrooms have softened, remove them from the liquid and set aside. Strain the mushroom liquid through a muslin-lined sieve to separate sand and grit, and reserve the liquid.

2. Heat the olive oil in a large saucepan and add the garlic, leeks and shallots and cook until golden (about 3 minutes). Add all the fresh mushrooms and cook over a very high heat until the mushrooms soften and their liquid evaporates (about 7 minutes). Reserve a few mushroom pieces for the garnish.

3. Transfer the leek and mushroom mixture to a preheated slow cooker set on high, then sprinkle with the flour and stir well to enable the flour to be absorbed. Add the stock and the porcini mushrooms together with the reserved liquid. Stir to combine. Cook for 2 hours.

4. Add the cream, then turn to low and cook for a further 30 minutes or until slightly thickened. Add half the parsley and the basil and oregano and season to taste with salt and freshly ground black pepper. To serve, ladle into individual bowls sprinkle with extra parsley, reserved mushrooms, some nutmeg and a small dollop of extra cream if desired.

German potato soup with cauliflower & caraway

SERVES 6

1. Cut 2in (5cm) lengths off the end of each spring onion. Using a sharp knife, slice these into thin strips, keeping one end intact to hold the strips together. Plunge the strips into a bowl of iced water and set aside until they curl (about 1 hour). Slice the remaining spring onion.

2. Then heat the olive oil in a slow cooker on a high setting and add the remaining spring onion and the cauliflower florets, potatoes and caraway seeds and cook for 50 minutes.

3. Add the stock and bring the soup to the simmer for 2 hours, then process with a food processor or hand-held blender until smooth. Add the reserved small cauliflower florets and simmer for 45 minutes. Serve the soup with a dollop of yoghurt, a sprinkling of caraway seeds and the spring onion curls.

1 bunch scallions (spring onions)
2 tablespoons olive oil
1 medium cauliflower head, cut into
  florets (reserve small florets)
21oz (600g) desiree potatoes, peeled,
  diced
1 teaspoon caraway seeds, plus extra
  for garnish
6 cups vegetable stock
2 tablespoons natural yoghurt

Roma tomato, lentil & basil soup

SERVES 4

1. Rinse the lentils, drain and add them to a large saucepan of boiling water. Simmer, covered, for 25 minutes or until tender. Drain, rinse and set aside.

2. Meanwhile, place the tomatoes in a bowl, cover with boiling water, leave for 30 seconds, then drain. Remove the skins, deseed and chop.

3. In a slow cooker on high, add the onions and stir in the tomatoes, tomato purée, stock, bay leaf and pepper. Cover and bring to the simmer. Simmer for 2¼ hours.

4. Remove and discard the bay leaf, then purée the soup until smooth in a food processor or with a hand-held blender. Stir in the lentils and chopped basil, then reheat. Serve garnished with the fresh basil leaves.

½ cup brown lentils
36oz (1kg) Roma tomatoes
2 onions, diced
2 tablespoons sun-dried tomato
  purée
3 cups vegetable stock
1 bay leaf
freshly ground black pepper
3 tablespoons chopped fresh basil,
  plus extra leaves to garnish

Spanish pea soup

SERVES 8

2 cups dried green split peas, rinsed
3 cups water
1 tablespoon olive oil
1 tablespoon Spanish paprika
2 cups diced onion
1 clove garlic, crushed
1 cup chopped green bell pepper
(capsicum)
¾ cup thinly sliced carrot
3 medium red potatoes, peeled,
cubed
7 cups chicken or vegetable stock
salt and freshly ground black pepper
14¾oz (420g) canned sweet corn
½ bunch fresh chives, chopped to
garnish

1. Place split peas in a large pot, cover with the water and bring to the boil. Simmer for 2 minutes then remove from the heat and cover. Let stand for 1 hour.

2. Heat the oil in a large saucepan and add the Spanish paprika, onion and garlic and sauté for 5 minutes until the mixture is fragrant and the onions have softened.

3. Add the green pepper, carrot and potato. Toss the vegetables thoroughly with the onion mixture until well coated, then continue to cook for 10 minutes, stirring thoroughly during the cooking.

4. Transfer to a slow cooker set on high and add the stock, split peas and salt and pepper to taste. Cook for 4 hours or until the split peas are very tender.

5. Reserve ½ cup of corn, then add the remainder to the soup and purée the soup until thick and smooth. Return the soup to the slow cooker and cook for a further 30 minutes. Serve scattered with a few corn kernels and some chopped chives on top.

Sienese bean soup

SERVES 8

*7oz (200g) dried red kidney beans,
  soaked overnight*
1 cup vegetable stock
3 cups water
¼ cup olive oil
2 carrots, diced
2 sticks celery, sliced
3 courgettes (zucchini), sliced
*15oz (425g) canned crushed
  tomatoes*
½ cup dry white wine
3 cloves garlic, crushed
2 bay leaves
8 cups chicken stock
9oz (250g) cabbage, sliced
2 tablespoons chopped fresh basil
2 tablespoons chopped fresh parsley
freshly ground black pepper

1. Drain beans, put in a saucepan and add vegetable stock and water. Bring to the boil and boil vigorously for 10 minutes. Lower heat and simmer for 1 hour.

2. Meanwhile, in a slow cooker set on high, add oil, carrots, celery, courgette, tomatoes, wine, garlic and bay leaves and cook for 1 hour.

3. Drain the red kidney beans and add to slow cooker with chicken stock. Cook for a further 2 hours.

4. Add cabbage and cook for 30 minutes more. Serve topped with chopped basil and parsley and cracked black pepper.

Chicken & leek soup with herb dumplings

SERVES 6

1. Place the chicken, onion, carrot and bundle of herbs in a slow cooker with the hot water. Cover and cook for 2 hours on high, then strain the stock and skim off any fat. Finely chop the chicken, discarding the skin and bones.

2. Heat half of the butter in a large saucepan, add the potatoes and two-thirds of the leeks, cover and cook for 10 minutes. Transfer to the slow cooker and add 4 cups of the stock and season. Cook for 50 minutes, until vegetables have softened. Blend in a food processor or with a hand-held blender until smooth, return to the slow cooker, then stir in the cooked chicken.

3. Make the dumplings while finishing the soup. Mix together the flour, bicarbonate of soda, breadcrumbs, butter, herbs and seasoning. Stir in water, then shape into 12 dumplings. Cook in simmering salted water for 15 minutes.

4. Add the rest of the butter and the chicken breast and the remaining leek. Cook for 2 hours, adding more stock if necessary. Remove from the heat and stir in the fresh tarragon and cream. To serve, divide between 6 bowls, drain the dumplings and add 2 to each bowl.

4 chicken cutlets
1 onion, chopped
1 carrot, chopped
*herb bundle made up of fresh
    tarragon, parsley and a bay leaf*
6 cups hot water
2oz (60g) butter
*10½oz (300g) potatoes, peeled,
    diced*
3 large leeks, sliced
salt and freshly ground black pepper
*2 boneless skinless chicken breasts,
    cut into small pieces*
2 teaspoons chopped fresh tarragon
5fl oz (145ml) light cream

DUMPLINGS

4oz (125g) all-purpose (plain) flour
½ teaspoon bicarbonate of soda
1oz (30g) fresh white breadcrumbs
1¾oz (50g) butter
*3 tablespoons chopped fresh herbs,
    such as tarragon, parsley or chives*
salt and freshly ground black pepper
⅓ cup water

Savoury pumpkin soup

SERVES 6–8

1. With the exception of parsley and cream, combine all ingredients in a slow cooker and cook for 6½ hours on low.
2. Remove bay leaf. Process the mixture a cupful at a time in a food processor.
3. Return mixture to slow cooker and reheat for 15 minutes. Add cream and allow to warm through.
4. Serve sprinkled with fresh parsley.

36oz (1kg) pumpkin, peeled, diced
14fl oz (400ml) canned tomato juice
1 tablespoon raw sugar
8 cups water
salt and freshly ground black pepper
1 bay leaf
few drops of Tabasco sauce
2 chicken stock cubes
½ cup pouring cream
2 tablespoons chopped fresh parsley

Sweet potato & rosemary soup

SERVES 4–6

2 tablespoons olive oil
2 cloves garlic, crushed
1 medium onion, chopped
3 tablespoons chopped fresh
  rosemary
2 tablespoons puréed semi-dried
  tomato
1 medium carrot, sliced
1 large potato, sliced
24oz (700g) sweet potato, sliced
4 cups chicken stock
salt and freshly ground black pepper

1. Heat the oil in a saucepan, add the garlic, onion and one-third of the rosemary, and cook on a medium heat for 5 minutes. Add the semi-dried tomato purée and cook for 1 minute.

2. Add the carrot, potato and sweet potato, and cook for a further 6 minutes.

3. Transfer to slow cooker set on high and add the stock and salt and pepper. Cook for 5 hours, or until the vegetables are soft.

4. Purée the soup in a food processor, then return to the slow cooker. Add the remaining rosemary and heat through before serving.

Indian spiced potato & onion soup

SERVES 4

1 tablespoon vegetable oil
1 onion, finely chopped
⅓in (1cm) piece fresh ginger, peeled,
  finely diced
2 large potatoes, cut into ⅓in (1cm)
  pieces
2 teaspoons ground cumin
2 teaspoons ground coriander
½ teaspoon ground turmeric
1 teaspoon ground cinnamon
2 tablespoons cold water
4 cups chicken stock
salt and freshly ground black pepper
1 tablespoon natural yoghurt to
  garnish

1. Heat the oil in a large saucepan. Cook onion and ginger for 5 minutes or until softened. Add the potatoes and cook for another 5 minutes, stirring often.

2. Mix the cumin, coriander, turmeric and cinnamon with cold water to make a paste. Add to the onion and potatoes and fry for 2 minutes, stirring well to release flavours.

3. Transfer the potato and spice mixture to a heated slow cooker set on a high setting. Add the stock and season to taste. Bring to the simmer and cover, then cook for 3 hours or until the potato is tender. Blend until smooth in a food processor or with a hand-held blender. Return to the slow cooker and heat through, then adjusting the seasoning again. Serve garnished with the yoghurt and more pepper.

TIP: This delicately spiced soup makes a great start to an Indian meal. It also makes a satisfying snack on its own, served with warm naan bread and a salad.

Roasted tomato, red pepper & bread soup

SERVES 4

1. Lightly oil a baking dish, place tomatoes and bell peppers in the dish and bake in a moderate oven for 20 minutes (or until the skins have blistered). After 15 minutes add the garlic, onion, cumin and coriander for the last 5 minutes. Set aside to cool, then remove the tomatoes and bell peppers, take off their skins and roughly chop.

2. Heat a slow cooker on a high setting and add all of the mixture from the bottom of the baking dish. Add tomatoes, bell peppers and stock and cook for 2 hours. Add bread, balsamic vinegar and salt and pepper, and cook for a further 50 minutes.

2 tablespoons olive oil
36oz (1kg) Roma tomatoes
2 red bell peppers (capsicums)
3 cloves garlic, crushed
2 onions, finely diced
2 teaspoons ground cumin
1 teaspoon ground coriander
4 cups chicken stock
2 slices white bread, crusts removed
   and torn into pieces
1 tablespoon balsamic vinegar
salt and freshly ground black pepper

seafood

Seafood casserole

SERVES 4–6

1 tablespoon olive oil
1 medium onion, roughly chopped
1 leek, finely chopped
2 cloves garlic, crushed
2 cups canned tomatoes
2 bay leaves
1 tablespoon chopped fresh parsley
¼ cup dry white wine
salt and freshly ground black pepper
36oz (1kg) assorted fish and seafood
2 tablespoons chopped fresh oregano
*   to garnish*

1. Heat the oil in a frying pan, add onion, leek and garlic and cook for 5 minutes until softened.

2. Transfer to a slow cooker set on high and add the tomatoes, bay leaves, parsley, wine, salt and pepper. Bring to the simmer, cover and cook for 50 minutes.

3. Stir in any firm-fleshed fish and cook for 25 minutes.

4. Stir in the soft-fleshed fish, placing the shellfish on the top. Cover with a lid and continue cooking for 40 minutes (until the fish is tender).

5. Serve garnished with the oregano.

TIP: Suitable fish and seafood include red mullet, monkfish, sea bream, cod, calamari, mussels, shelled shrimp and clams.

Bouillabaisse

SERVES 6

6lb 10oz (3kg) mixed fish and
  seafood, including firm white fish
  fillets, shrimp (prawn), mussels,
  crab and calamari rings
¼ cup olive oil
2 cloves garlic, crushed
2 large onions, chopped
2 leeks, sliced
2 x 14oz (400g) canned tomatoes
⅔ cup fish stock
1 tablespoon chopped fresh thyme or
  1 teaspoon dried thyme
2 tablespoons chopped fresh basil or
  1½ teaspoons dried basil
2 tablespoons chopped fresh parsley
2 bay leaves
2 tablespoons finely grated orange
  rind
1 teaspoon saffron threads
⅔ cup dry white wine
freshly ground black pepper

1. Remove the bones and skin from the fish fillets and cut into ¾in (2cm) cubes. Peel and devein the shrimp, leaving the tails intact. Scrub and remove the beards from the mussels. Cut the crab into quarters. Set aside.

2. Heat a slow cooker on a high setting, then add the oil, garlic, onions, leeks, tomatoes and stock and cook for 1½ hours. Add the thyme, basil, parsley, bay leaves, orange rind, saffron and wine. Cook for 30 minutes.

3. Add the fish and crab and cook for 1 hour. Add the remaining seafood and cook for 1 hour longer or until all fish and seafood are cooked. Season to taste with black pepper.

Braised fish with lemon

SERVES 4

1. Remove heads from fish, then scale and clean well. Season cavities with salt and pepper, and place slices of tomato and lemon in each cavity. Grease bowl of a slow cooker with olive oil. Place fish in the slow cooker, side by side, and season with salt and pepper. Top with 2 slices of lemon per fish and a drizzle of olive oil. Cover and cook on low for 1 hour.

2. Just before serving cut the butter into small cubes and scatter over the top of each piece of fish before covering again. After 10 minutes carefully remove the fish with a large spatula and arrange on a hot serving dish.

3. Pour the remaining liquid from the slow cooker over the fish. Garnish with a scattering of fresh parsley leaves.

2 whole bream or pearl perch
salt and freshly ground black pepper
1 tomato, sliced
2 lemons, sliced
olive oil
1¾oz (50g) butter
fresh parsley leaves to garnish

Slow fish stew on rosemary mash

SERVES 4

1. To make the rosemary mash, remove the leaves from the rosemary sprig. Place the leaves and the oil in a small saucepan over a low heat and heat until warm. Remove the pan from the heat and set aside to allow the flavours to develop. If possible, do this several hours in advance; the longer the leaves steep in the oil, the more pronounced the flavour becomes. Boil potatoes until tender. Drain well. Add milk and rosemary oil. Mash the potatoes and season with white pepper.

2. Meanwhile, heat a slow cooker on high. Add the oil, leek, garlic, oregano, mushrooms, celery, courgettes, tomatoes and wine. Cook for 40 minutes.

3. Stir in the tomato paste. Cook for 30 minutes or until the mixture starts to thicken.

4. Reduce the heat to low and add the fish. Cook for 2 hours until the fish is just cooked; take care not to overcook or the fish will fall apart. Stir in the basil and parsley. Serve with the mash.

2 teaspoons olive oil
1 leek, diced, washed
1 clove garlic, crushed
1 teaspoon dried oregano
4 field mushrooms, sliced
1 stick celery, sliced
2 cups canned no-added-salt diced tomatoes
2 courgettes (zucchini), sliced
½ cup dry white wine
1 tablespoon no-added-salt tomato paste
21oz (600g) firm white fish fillets
1 tablespoon chopped fresh basil
1 tablespoon chopped fresh parsley

ROSEMARY MASH
1 sprig fresh rosemary
2 teaspoons olive oil
2 large potatoes, peeled, quartered
¼ cup low-fat milk, warmed
ground white pepper

Fish with brown butter sauce

SERVES 6

36oz (1kg) firm, white-fleshed fish
3 teaspoons salt
1 tablespoon white wine vinegar
1 bay leaf
1 onion, sliced
4 whole black peppercorns
few stalks of parsley
grated rind of 1 lemon
2 tablespoons chopped fresh dill
1 tablespoon capers

BROWN BUTTER SAUCE
2oz (60g) butter
2 tablespoons white wine vinegar

1. Wash the fish and cut into serving pieces.
2. Place in a slow cooker and cover with cold water. Add salt, white wine vinegar, bay leaf, onion and peppercorns and cook for 2 hours and 20 minutes on low.
3. Lift with a fish slice onto a cutting board. Scrape away the skin from both sides and carefully remove larger bones. Transfer to a heated serving dish and keep hot while making the sauce. Sprinkle parsley, lemon rind, dill and capers over fish.
4. To make the sauce, heat a small frying pan, add the butter and heat carefully until it begins to turn brown, being careful not to burn it. Pour over fish. Add the white wine vinegar to pan and reduce by half – this only takes a second. Pour over fish as well and serve immediately with lemon wedges.

Shellfish stew

SERVES 6

26½oz (750g) live lobster or
  2 frozen lobster tails
6 tablespoons olive oil
17½oz (500g) shrimp (prawns),
  shelled
17½oz (500g) cod or other firm-
  fleshed fish steak, cut into bite-
  size pieces
9oz (250g) whole small calamari,
  cleaned
1 small onion, chopped
1 red bell pepper (capsicum),
  chopped
3 cloves garlic, crushed
3 medium tomatoes, peeled,
  deseeded, chopped
¼ teaspoon saffron threads
2 tablespoons minced parsley
1 bay leaf
½ teaspoon dried thyme
¼ teaspoon chilli flakes
¾ cup dry white wine
¼ cup lemon juice
salt and freshly ground black pepper
12 very small clams, thoroughly
  scrubbed
12 mussels, scrubbed, de-bearded

1. As close as possible to the time you are going to cook the lobster, have the fishmonger cut the claws and tail from it and break them into serving-size pieces.

2. Heat the oil in a large frying pan and quickly sauté lobster over high heat for 3 minutes. Remove and set aside.

3. In the frying pan on a medium heat cook the shrimp and fish for 3½ minutes. Remove and set aside.

4. Add calamari, onion, pepper and garlic and cook for 3½ minutes. Transfer mixture to a slow cooker set on high and stir in tomatoes, saffron, parsley, bay leaf, thyme and chilli flakes and cook for 25 minutes. Stir in wine, lemon juice and salt and pepper and cook for 20 minutes. Add reserved seafood, cover and simmer for 30 minutes longer.

5. Meanwhile, in a covered pan, steam clams and mussels with 2 cups of water over high heat. As clams and mussels open, remove them and add to casserole. Serve immediately.

Kedgeree

SERVES 4

1. Place smoked fish in saucepan, cover with cold water and bring slowly to the simmer. Cook for 6 minutes, drain and flake.
2. Melt butter in a large frying pan over a medium heat and fry onion until soft. Add curry powder and cook, stirring, for 2 minutes. Add rice and leeks and fry gently for 5 minutes, stirring, until rice is translucent yet slightly brown in colour.
3. Place rice mixture in a slow cooker and add boiling water, dashi stock and flaked fish. Gently stir to combine all ingredients, cover and cook on high for 2 hours.
4. When ready to serve add cream and eggs and toss gently with a fork. Season to taste with freshly ground black pepper. Sprinkle with parsley. Serve with lemon wedges if desired.

17½oz (500g) smoked trout or cod
1 leek, diced, washed
1oz (30g) butter
1 onion, finely sliced
1 teaspoon curry powder
1 cup basmati rice
2 cups boiling water
1 sachet Japanese dashi stock
2 tablespoons cream
2 hard-boiled eggs, coarsely chopped
freshly ground black pepper
2 tablespoons chopped fresh parsley

Sour shrimp curry

SERVES 4

1. Place the coconut milk, shrimp paste, curry paste, lemongrass, chillies, cumin and coriander in a slow cooker set on high and bring to a simmer. Stirring occasionally, cook for 1 hour.
2. Stir the shrimp, cucumbers, bamboo shoots and tamarind mixture into the coconut milk mixture and cook, stirring occasionally, for 45 minutes or until the shrimp are cooked.
3. Serve with steamed rice.

2 cups coconut milk
1 teaspoon shrimp paste
2 tablespoons Thai green curry paste
1 stalk lemongrass, finely chopped
or ½ teaspoon dried lemongrass,
soaked in hot water until soft
2 fresh green chillies, chopped
1 tablespoon ground cumin
1 tablespoon ground coriander
17½oz (500g) large uncooked
shrimp (prawns), shelled,
deveined (leaving tails intact)
3 cucumbers, halved and sliced
4oz (115g) canned bamboo shoots,
drained
1 tablespoon tamarind concentrate,
dissolved in 3 tablespoons hot
water

Creole shrimp

SERVES 4

1 tablespoon olive oil
1 large onion, diced
1 clove garlic, crushed
1 small green bell pepper (capsicum),
  diced
3 sticks celery, diced
1 cup tomato pasta sauce
14oz (400g) canned whole peeled
  tomatoes
1 teaspoon smoked paprika
1 teaspoon salt
¼ teaspoon black pepper
grated rind of 1 lemon
17½oz (500g) uncooked king shrimp
  (prawns), shelled, deveined
  (leaving tails intact)

1. Heat the oil in a large frying pan. Add the onion and cook over a medium heat for 2 minutes. Add the garlic and cook for a further minute, stirring constantly.

2. Combine onion and garlic and all ingredients, except shrimp, in a slow cooker and cook on high for 2½ hours.

3. Add the shrimp, stir and reduce heat. Continue to cook on low for another hour.

Goan-style fish & coconut curry

SERVES 4

2 tomatoes
2 cardamom pods, bruised
1 teaspoon ground coriander
1 teaspoon ground cumin
1 teaspoon ground cinnamon
1 teaspoon hot chilli powder
½ teaspoon ground turmeric
2 tablespoons water
2 tablespoons vegetable oil
1 onion, finely chopped
1 clove garlic, finely chopped
1in (25mm) piece fresh root ginger,
    finely chopped
14fl oz (400ml) coconut milk
24oz (700g) skinless white fish fillet,
    such as haddock or cod, cut into
    1in (25mm) chunks
salt to taste
fresh cilantro (coriander) leaves to
    garnish

1. Place tomatoes in a bowl, cover with boiling water and leave to stand for 30 seconds. Peel, then finely chop.

2. Crush cardamom seeds using a mortar and pestle. Add coriander, cumin, cinnamon, chilli powder, turmeric and water and mix to a paste. Set aside.

3. Heat oil in a large heavy-based saucepan. Cook onion, garlic and ginger for 3 minutes or until softened. Add spice paste, mix well and cook for 1 minute, stirring constantly.

4. Transfer to a slow cooker on a high setting, pour in coconut milk and bring to the simmer for 30 minutes. Add fish, tomatoes and salt. Partly cover and cook for a further 45 minutes or until fish turns opaque and is cooked through. Garnish with cilantro leaves and serve on a bed of rice.

Slowfood paella

SERVES 8

1. Preheat slow cooker to a high heat level. Add the oil and the onions and stir, then add the garlic, thyme, lemon rind and tomatoes and cook for 15 minutes.

2. Add the rice and saffron mixture and warmed stock. Simmer, stirring occasionally, for 1½ hours or until the rice has absorbed almost all the liquid.

3. Stir in the peas, peppers and mussels and cook for 20 minutes. Add the fish, shrimp and scallops and cook for 20 minutes. Stir in the calamari and parsley and cook for 20 minutes longer or until the seafood is cooked.

1 tablespoon olive oil

2 onions, chopped

2 cloves garlic, crushed

1 tablespoon fresh thyme leaves

2 teaspoons finely grated lemon rind

4 ripe tomatoes, chopped

2½ cups short-grain white rice

pinch saffron threads, soaked in 2 cups water

5 cups chicken or fish stock

10½oz (300g) fresh or frozen peas

2 red bell peppers (capsicums), chopped

36oz (1kg) mussels, scrubbed, de-bearded

17½oz (500g) firm white fish fillets, chopped

10oz (285g) peeled uncooked shrimp (prawns)

7oz (200g) scallops

3 calamari, cleaned, sliced

1 tablespoon chopped fresh parsley

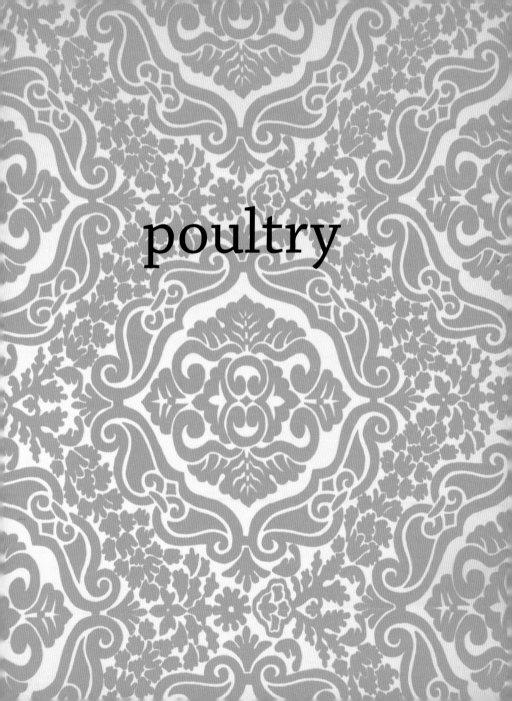

poultry

Spanish chicken with chorizo

SERVES 4

8 chicken drumsticks
2 tablespoons olive oil
1 onion, sliced
2 cloves garlic, crushed
1 red bell pepper (capsicum), sliced
1 yellow bell pepper (capsicum), sliced
2 teaspoons paprika
3 tablespoons dry sherry or dry vermouth
2 cups canned chopped tomatoes
1 bay leaf
1 strip orange rind
2 chorizo sausages, sliced
⅓ cup pitted black olives
salt and freshly ground black pepper

1. Place the chicken in a large non-stick frying pan and cook without oil for 12 minutes, turning occasionally, until golden. Remove the chicken and set aside. Drain any fat from the pan and discard.

2. Add the oil to the pan and cook the onion, garlic and peppers for 3 minutes, until softened.

3. Transfer the mixture to a slow cooker set on low, add the chicken and the paprika, sherry or vermouth, tomatoes, bay leaf and orange rind. Bring to temperature and cook for 5 hours.

4. Add the chorizo and olives and cook for a further 30 minutes, then season.

TIP: Packed with Mediterranean flavours, this casserole is equally good with rice or crusty bread. You can use stock or orange juice instead of the sherry or vermouth.

Chicken curry with jasmine rice

SERVES 4

2 cups reduced-fat coconut milk
1 cup reduced-salt chicken stock
2 tablespoons green curry paste
3 kaffir lime leaves, shredded
7oz (200g) chopped pumpkin
4 skinless chicken breast fillets, diced
4oz (115g) canned bamboo shoots,
 drained
3½oz (100g) snake beans, chopped
7oz (200g) broccoli, cut into florets
1 tablespoon fish sauce
1 tablespoon grated palm sugar
2 tablespoons torn fresh Thai basil
 leaves

JASMINE RICE
1½ cups jasmine rice
2 stalks lemongrass, halved
4 cups water

1. Combine coconut milk, stock, curry paste and lime leaves in a slow cooker on high. Cook until the sauce begins to thicken. Add the pumpkin and cook for 20 minutes or until it starts to soften.

2. Add the chicken and bamboo shoots and cook for 1 hour. Add the beans, broccoli, fish sauce and palm sugar and cook until the vegetables are tender, for approximately 1 more hour. Then stir through the basil leaves.

3. Meanwhile, to make the jasmine rice, put the rice, lemongrass and water in a pot. Bring to boil and cook over a high heat until steam holes appear in the top of the rice. Reduce the heat to low, cover and cook for 10 minutes or until all the liquid is absorbed and the rice is tender. Transfer the rice to bowls, spoon over the curry and serve.

Chicken mexicana

SERVES 6

1. In a slow cooker on a low heat setting mix all ingredients except the sour cream and parsley. Cook for 7½ hours.
2. Carefully transfer chicken to a serving dish and keep warm. Meanwhile, turn the slow cooker onto high. Simmer the sauce for 20 minutes, add the sour cream and the parsley and pour over the chicken. Serve with rice.

3lb 5oz (1.5kg) whole chicken
1½oz (40g) butter
2 tablespoons olive oil
2 large onions, sliced
2 cloves garlic, crushed
1 green bell pepper (capsicum), sliced
1 red chilli, diced
1 teaspoon dill seeds
7oz (200g) canned tomatoes
2 tablespoons tomato paste
5fl oz (150ml) chicken stock
2 ears fresh corn, corn cut from
    the cob
4 tablespoons sour cream
1 tablespoon chopped fresh parsley

Fricasseed chicken with vinegar

SERVES 4

1. Remove any excess fat from the chicken fillets and cut each into 4 pieces. In a wide heavy-based pan, heat the olive oil and brown the chicken pieces all over, seasoning well with pepper. Transfer to a plate and keep warm.

2. Heat the pan over a low heat and add garlic, rosemary and anchovies. Cook and stir until the mixture is aromatic.

3. Transfer the mixture and the chicken to a slow cooker set on a high heat. Add the white wine vinegar, cover and simmer for about 1½ hours until the chicken is tender.

4. Just before removing from the heat, stir in the balsamic vinegar, which will give the dish a great lift. Serve with silverbeet and potatoes roasted in olive oil with a few sprigs of rosemary and olives.

1lb 15oz (900g) chicken thigh fillets
¼ cup olive oil
freshly ground black pepper
2 large cloves garlic, chopped
2 teaspoons chopped fresh rosemary
5 anchovy fillets, chopped
½ cup white wine vinegar
2 tablespoons balsamic vinegar
20 Kalamata olives, to serve

American chicken casserole

SERVES 4

2 tablespoons oil
8 chicken drumsticks
salt and freshly ground black pepper
4 onions, sliced
10½fl oz (300ml) chicken stock
½ teaspoon chilli powder
2 tablespoons all-purpose (plain)
    flour
2 x 14oz (400g) canned tomatoes
1 x 14oz (400g) canned red kidney
    beans, rinsed, drained
1¾oz (50g) butter

1. Heat the oil in a large frying pan over medium heat. Add the chicken, season and cook until browned. Add the onions and fry for 1 minute.

2. Heat stock in a small saucepan until simmering.

3. In a preheated slow cooker set on high, sprinkle the chilli powder and flour. Slowly add the stock, stirring constantly. Transfer chicken and onions to slow cooker and add the tomatoes, beans and butter. Cover and cook for 3½ hours on high.

Portuguese jugged chicken

SERVES 4

2oz (60g) butter
8 small onions, peeled
3lb 5oz (1.5kg) whole chicken
3 tomatoes, cut into wedges
3½oz (100g) smoked ham or bacon,
    diced
2 bay leaves
2 cloves garlic, crushed
2 teaspoons Dijon mustard
¾ cup dry white wine
¼ cup port wine
2 tablespoons brandy
salt and freshly ground black pepper

1. Melt ⅔oz (20g) butter in a large heavy-based frying pan over medium heat. Add onions and cook for 2 minutes, stirring constantly. Brush chicken all over with the remaining butter. Add chicken to pan and cook for 4 minutes.

2. In a slow cooker set on low, arrange tomatoes, ham or bacon and bay leaves over base of dish. Add the contents of the frying pan and splash the pan with a little of the white wine and add to the slow cooker as well.

3. Blend together garlic, mustard, remaining white wine, port wine, brandy, salt and pepper. Pour over chicken, cover and cook for 7 hours.

TIP: As an alternative you can carefully remove the ceramic insert with the jugged chicken in the last 15 minutes of cooking and put in an oven, preheated to 400°F (200°C). Bake with the lid removed to brown the chicken. Cut the chicken into pieces and serve with crispy potatoes and salad.

Slow chicken with ricotta, arugula & red peppers

SERVES 4

1. Combine the ricotta, rocket, pine nuts, bell pepper and salt and pepper in a small bowl and mix together until smooth.

2. Place 1–2 tablespoons of ricotta mixture under the skin of each chicken breast.

3. Place the chicken breasts in a slow cooker set on high, sprinkle with more salt and pepper, place 1 teaspoon of butter on each breast and pour the stock around the chicken. Cook for 2 hours on high. Serve the chicken with juices and a rocket salad.

7oz (200g) fresh ricotta cheese
1 cup chopped arugula (rocket)
¼ cup toasted pine nuts
3½oz (100g) chargrilled marinated
    bell pepper (capsicum), chopped
salt and freshly ground black pepper
4 chicken breasts, skin on; each 6oz
    (170g)
⅔oz (20g) butter
1 cup chicken stock

Duck with cherries & radicchio

SERVES 4

1. Combine the duck and onion in the slow cooker. Pour over the stock, cherries and half of the cherry juice. Sprinkle with grated lemon rind and seasoning. Cover and cook for 4 hours on high.
2. Remove duck from slow cooker. Cut duck into pieces, then cover and keep warm. Drain cherries from slow cooker and retain 3–4 tablespoons of liquid.
3. Pour remaining cherry juice and retained liquid into a saucepan. Make the cornflour into a paste with the blackcurrant syrup, stir it through the liquid and bring to a boil. Reduce liquid by half and drizzle over the duck.
4. To prepare the gremolata, combine all ingredients in a small bowl.
5. Serve pieces of duck and cherries in radicchio leaves, sprinkled with gremolata.

1 duck
1 onion, chopped
10½fl oz (300ml) chicken stock
15oz (450g) canned black cherries
finely grated rind of 1 lemon
salt and freshly ground black pepper
1 tablespoon cornflour
1 tablespoon blackcurrant syrup
12 radicchio leaves, washed

GREMOLATA
rind of 1 lemon, finely diced
2 cloves garlic, finely diced
¼ cup chopped fresh parsley

Moroccan-style chicken wings

SERVES 4

2 tablespoons vegetable oil
36oz (1kg) chicken wings
1 large onion, finely chopped
1 clove garlic, crushed
1½ teaspoons grated fresh ginger
½ teaspoon ground turmeric
½ teaspoon ground cumin
1 cinnamon stick
¼ cup cider vinegar
2 cups apricot nectar
salt and freshly ground black pepper
3oz (90g) dried prunes, pitted
3oz (90g) dried apricots
1 tablespoon honey
¼ cup lemon juice
fresh parsley sprigs to garnish

1. Heat the oil in a large saucepan. Add the chicken wings, a few at a time, and brown lightly on both sides. Remove to a plate as they brown.

2. Add the onion and cook for 2 minutes. Stir in the garlic and cook for a further minute.

3. Transfer the onion and garlic to a slow cooker on a low setting. Add the chicken, ginger and spices. Stir and turn the wings to coat with spices. Add the vinegar and apricot nectar and season to taste. Cover and cook for 6 hours.

4. Add the prunes, apricots, honey and lemon juice. Cover and simmer for 2 more hours and then remove lid, turn to high and simmer uncovered for 35 minutes. If a thicker sauce is desired, remove the wings and fruit to a serving platter and simmer until the sauce reduces and thickens. Pour the sauce over the wings. Serve immediately on a bed of steamed couscous or rice, garnished with a sprig of parsley.

Chicken marengo

serves 6

3lb 13oz (1.75kg) chicken pieces
salt and freshly ground black pepper
2 tablespoons all-purpose (plain)
  flour
1 tablespoon olive oil
⅔oz (20g) butter
2 cloves garlic, crushed
1 bouquet garni
¾ cup hot water
2 tablespoons brandy
2 large tomatoes, peeled, chopped
12 button mushrooms, sliced
2 tablespoons chopped fresh parsley
  to garnish

1. Season the chicken pieces with salt and pepper and sprinkle with half of the flour. Heat oil and butter in a large heavy-based saucepan. Add the chicken and cook over a medium heat until golden, turning frequently.
2. Transfer the chicken to a slow cooker set on low and add garlic, bouquet garni, hot water, brandy, tomatoes and mushrooms. Cover and cook for 6 hours.
3. Approximately 20 minutes before serving combine remaining flour with a little water to make a smooth paste. Stir through chicken to thicken the sauce if necessary. Sprinkle with chopped parsley and serve with steamed rice.

Hunter's chicken

1. Season chicken pieces with salt and pepper. Place the chicken pieces along with all the other ingredients, except cornflour and water, in a slow cooker. Stir well. Cover and cook on high for 3 hours.

2. Remove chicken pieces and keep warm. Make a smooth paste of cornflour and water and stir into slow cooker. Return chicken, cover and cook for 15 minutes until the gravy thickens. Serve with steamed couscous.

3lb 5oz (1.5kg) chicken pieces
salt and freshly ground black pepper
1 cinnamon stick
2 cloves garlic, chopped
1 green bell pepper (capsicum),
chopped
2 small onions, sliced
2 sticks celery, chopped
8 small mushrooms, sliced
¼ cup dry sherry
1 cup canned tomatoes, chopped
¼ cup cornflour
¼ cup water

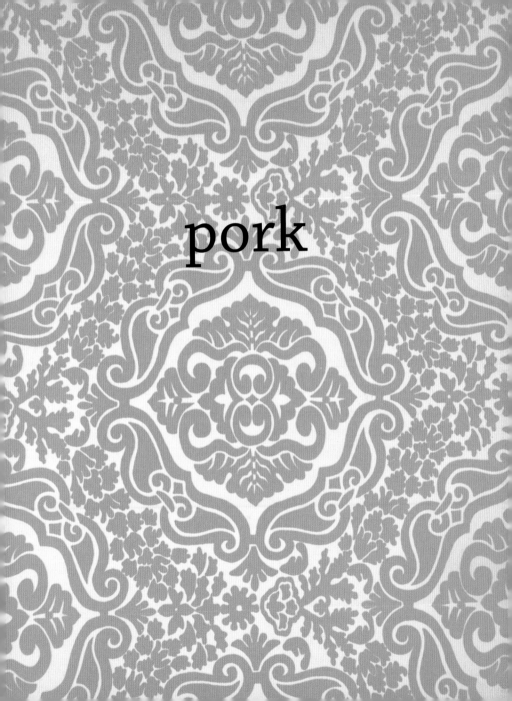

pork

Gingered roast pork

SERVES 6

3lb 5oz (1.5kg) pork loin or leg, well
   trimmed, tied with kitchen string
salt and freshly ground black pepper
3 Granny Smith apples, peeled,
   cored, quartered
1 tablespoon brown sugar
2 teaspoons ground ginger
1 teaspoon salt
1 tablespoon cornflour
1 tablespoon water

1. Rub pork rind with salt and pepper.
Arrange apples in base of slow cooker. Place
pork on top of apples.

2. Combine brown sugar, ginger and salt.
Spoon over top surface of pork. Cover and
cook on low for 7 hours.

3. Ten minutes before serving strain off 1
cup of liquid into a small saucepan. Blend
cornflour with water to make a smooth paste
and stir into liquid. Heat until thickened.
Remove string from the pork roll and carve.
Serve with sauce, accompanied by the
apples and freshly steamed vegetables.

Indonesian pork spare ribs

SERVES 4

26½oz (750g) pork spare ribs
1½ tablespoons peanut oil
1 teaspoon ground coriander
½ teaspoon ground cumin
½ teaspoon freshly ground black
   pepper
2 tablespoons soy sauce
1 tablespoon tamarind concentrate
1 teaspoon brown sugar
¼ cup water

PASTE
2 French shallots, chopped
2 cloves garlic
2 teaspoons finely grated fresh ginger
¼ cup water

1. Pound the paste ingredients in a mortar and pestle or combine in a small food processor.

2. Chop spare ribs in half. Heat 1 tablespoon of oil in a wok or medium frying pan. Add spare ribs in 2 batches and fry for 2–3 minutes or until ribs are golden and crisp. Remove and set aside.

3. Heat remaining oil and add paste. Cook for 2 minutes, stirring constantly. Add coriander, cumin, black pepper, soy sauce, tamarind and sugar.

4. Turn all ingredients out into slow cooker set on a high heat setting. Return ribs to sauce, add water and cook for 4 hours, basting and turning every hour. Add a little extra water if sauce becomes too thick. Serve with Chinese greens and a side bowl of rice.

Pork cutlets with quince

SERVES 4

1. In a slow cooker set on a high heat setting, add white wine, garlic, onion and quince and cook with the lid on for 20 minutes, stirring occasionally.

2. Meanwhile, heat oil in a frying pan. Carefully fry pork cutlets on their sides, browning the pork rind only, for 2–3 minutes. Set meat aside.

3. Stir into slow cooker the orange juice, chicken stock, cinnamon stick and honey. Add the pork and turn down to a low heat setting and cook for 8 hours (or until sauce has thickened slightly). Stir in parsley, salt and pepper, and serve.

1 tablespoon olive oil
4 pork cutlets

SAUCE
½ cup dry white wine
1 clove garlic, crushed
1 medium red onion, sliced
1 medium quince, peeled, cored, cut
  into thin wedges
juice of 1 orange
⅓ cup chicken stock
1 cinnamon stick
1 tablespoon honey
1 tablespoon chopped fresh parsley
salt and freshly ground black pepper

Boston pork & beans

SERVES 4

1. Heat the oil in a large frying pan over medium heat. Add meat and cook until browned. Remove meat from pan. Cook onion for 3 minutes. Add garlic and cook for a further 2 minutes.
2. Layer beans, onions and tomatoes in a slow cooker. Top with meat and add the herbs (tied into a bouquet with kitchen string).
3. Mix together sugar, golden syrup, tomato paste, bitters, mustard, salt, pepper and tomato juice. Spoon over ingredients in slow cooker. Cover slow cooker and cook for 4 hours on high.

9oz (250g) dried haricot beans, soaked overnight, drained
2 tablespoons olive oil
17½oz (500g) bacon or ham hock, diced
1 large onion, chopped
1 clove garlic, crushed
14oz (400g) canned diced tomatoes
1 bay leaf
2 sprigs fresh thyme
1 sprig fresh marjoram
2 tablespoons dark brown sugar
1 tablespoon golden syrup
1 tablespoon tomato paste
2 teaspoons Angostura bitters
3 teaspoons Dijon mustard
salt and freshly ground black pepper
¼ cup tomato juice

Chorizo & lentil stew

SERVES 4

9oz (250g) brown lentils, rinsed
4 cups boiling water
4 tomatoes
3½ cups chicken stock
9oz (250g) chorizo sausage, chopped
1 red onion, sliced
2 garlic cloves, crushed
½ teaspoon dried crushed chillies
salt and freshly ground black pepper
chopped fresh flat-leaf parsley to
    garnish

1. Place the lentils and boiling water in a slow cooker set on high. Cook for 30 minutes, stirring occasionally. Meanwhile, place the tomatoes in a bowl and cover with boiling water. Leave for 30 seconds, then peel, remove the seeds and chop the flesh. Drain the lentils and return to slow cooker with ¼ cup fresh water and stock.

2. Put the chorizo into a large heavy-based frying pan and cook over a low heat until the fat starts to run out of the sausage. Increase the heat to high and cook, stirring frequently, for 8 minutes or until browned. Add the onions and cook for 2 more minutes.

3. Transfer chorizo and onion to the slow cooker, then stir in the chopped tomatoes, garlic and chillies. Season with salt and pepper and cook, covered, for 4 hours, until quite thick but not too dry. Garnish with parsley.

Swedish pork meatballs

SERVES 6

1½ cups white breadcrumbs
1 cup buttermilk
17½oz (500g) lean pork mince
9oz (250g) lean beef mince
2 eggs
1 medium onion, finely chopped
2 teaspoons salt
¾ teaspoon dill seeds
¼ teaspoon allspice
⅛ teaspoon ground nutmeg
2oz (60g) butter
1 cup chicken stock
½ cup dry white wine
freshly ground black pepper
1 cup cream
2 tablespoons fresh parsley leaves to
  garnish

1. Soak breadcrumbs in buttermilk for 5 minutes. Add meats, eggs, onion, salt, herbs and spices. Mix well, cover and refrigerate for 30 minutes.

2. Shape tablespoon quantities of mixture into balls.

3. Heat butter in a medium frying pan and cook meatballs until lightly browned.

4. Place meatballs into the slow cooker as they are browned. Add stock, wine and pepper. Cover and cook on low for 5 hours.

5. Approximately 20 minutes before serving turn the heat to high and add cream. Serve meatballs garnished with parsley and accompanied by crusty bread.

TIP: The meatballs will have a finer texture if the meats are minced together twice (ask your butcher to do this).

Braised pork with apples

1. Heat half of the oil in a large non-stick frying pan. Add the pork and cook each side for 3 minutes or until browned, then transfer to a slow cooker set on low.

2. Heat the remaining oil in pan and add the scallions and mushrooms and cook gently for 5 minutes or until softened. Add the flour and cook for 1 minute, stirring. Slowly add the stock and cider, stirring until smooth, then add the mustard and pepper. Bring to the boil and continue stirring for 2–3 minutes, until thickened slightly.

3. Place the apple slices on top of the pork steaks in the slow cooker and pour over the sauce. Cover and cook for 5 hours. Garnish with the parsley.

TIP: Pork goes beautifully with the slight tartness of cooked apples. In this succulent slow-cooked casserole, the cider brings out the taste of the apples even more.

1 tablespoon olive oil
4 pork medallions
4 scallions (spring onions), thinly
  sliced
7oz (200g) button mushrooms, sliced
1 tablespoon all-purpose (plain) flour
1 cup vegetable stock
½ cup dry cider
2 teaspoons Dijon or wholegrain
  mustard
freshly ground black pepper
2 large green apples, peeled, cored,
  sliced
fresh flat-leaf parsley to garnish

Mediterranean pork pot roast

SERVES 6–8

1. Combine diced onion, garlic, celery, oregano and bacon in a bowl. Lightly flour the pork with 1 tablespoon of flour, then rub with vegetable mixture.
2. Place the remaining sliced onion in a slow cooker. Place the pork on top of the onion. Cover and cook on low for 7½ hours.
3. Ten minutes before serving, remove pork from the cooker and keep warm. Thicken the juices in the cooker with the remaining tablespoon of flour. Slice pork and serve drizzled with juices.

2 onions, 1 finely diced and 1 sliced
2 cloves garlic, finely diced
1 large stick celery, finely diced
1 tablespoon finely chopped fresh oregano
1 rasher thick-cut bacon, finely diced
2 tablespoons all-purpose (plain) flour
4lb 6oz (2kg) pork loin roll roast

Tuscan sausage pot

SERVES 4

2 tablespoons olive oil
17½oz (500g) pork sausages
1 red onion, sliced
2 sticks celery, sliced
1 large carrot, diced
1 clove garlic, crushed
4 Roma tomatoes
½ cup dry white wine
salt and freshly ground black pepper
14oz (400g) canned cannellini
    beans, rinsed
4 cups water
1 teaspoon salt
7oz (200g) instant polenta
1oz (30g) butter
chopped fresh flat-leaf parsley to
    garnish

1. Heat 1 tablespoon of the oil in a large frying pan and cook the sausages for 5 minutes or until browned, turning occasionally. Remove from the pan. Add the remaining oil and cook the onion, celery, carrot and garlic for 3–4 minutes, until lightly coloured.

2. Meanwhile, put the tomatoes in a bowl and cover with boiling water. Leave for 30 seconds, then peel and cut the flesh into quarters.

3. Place the tomatoes, sausages and sautéed vegetables into a slow cooker set on high and add the wine and the seasoning. Cook for 2 hours.

4. Add the beans and cook for a further 1½ hours.

5. Just before the sausage pot is ready bring water to the boil in a large saucepan and add salt. Sprinkle in the polenta and stir for 5 minutes or until thick and smooth, then add the butter. Serve with the sausage pot, sprinkled with parsley.

TIP: This is the Italian version of bangers and mash. Polenta is used instead of potato and the sausages are cooked with lots of vegetables.

Portuguese pork with cumin

SERVES 4

3 cloves garlic, crushed
1 teaspoon ground cumin
finely grated rind of 1 lemon
2 tablespoons lemon juice
2 teaspoons Dijon mustard
½ cup dry white wine
¼ cup chopped fresh cilantro
  (coriander)
26½oz (750g) fillet pork, cut into
  ¾in (2cm) pieces
¼ cup olive oil
1 onion, sliced
¾ cup chicken stock
salt and freshly ground black pepper
cilantro (coriander) leaves to garnish

1. Mix together garlic, cumin, lemon rind, lemon juice, mustard, white wine and cilantro in a shallow bowl. Add pork and coat well in the mixture.

2. Heat 2 tablespoons of oil in a large frying pan over medium to high heat. Remove pork from marinade with a slotted spoon, reserving marinade. Add pork to frying pan and cook in batches until golden. Remove and set aside. Heat remaining oil and cook onion until soft.

3. Place pork and onion in a slow cooker set on low and add the remaining marinade and chicken stock. Cover and simmer for 4½ hours. Season with salt and pepper and garnish with cilantro leaves. Serve pork with lemon wedges and fried potatoes.

lamb

Irish stew

SERVES 4

2 large onions, sliced
36oz (1kg) lamb neck pieces
2 teaspoons mixed dried herbs
salt and freshly ground black pepper
2–3 large potatoes, peeled, sliced
2 cups chicken stock
1 tablespoon chopped fresh parsley
   to garnish

1.   Place one quarter of the onions in a slow cooker and place the lamb on top. Sprinkle with herbs and season well.

2.   Combine remaining onions and potatoes and place over lamb. Season well, pour over stock and cook for 5½ hours on high. Serve sprinkled with freshly chopped parsley and steamed vegetables.

African bobotie curry

SERVES 4

1 tablespoon vegetable oil
1 onion, finely chopped
2 thick slices of white bread, broken
    into pieces (crusts removed)
1¼ cups milk
17½oz (500g) lean lamb mince
2 tablespoons curry paste
2 cloves garlic, crushed
salt and freshly ground black pepper
juice of ½ lemon
1¾oz (50g) dried apricots, chopped
1¾oz (50g) raisins
2oz (60g) flaked almonds
2 eggs

1. Heat the oil in a large heavy-based frying pan, add the onion and fry for 5 minutes to soften. Place the bread in a bowl with the milk and leave to soak.

2. Meanwhile, add the lamb to the pan and cook for 10 minutes or until browned, breaking it up with a wooden spoon. Transfer the lamb to a slow cooker set on high and add the curry paste, garlic and seasoning and cook for 30 minutes. Add the lemon juice, apricots and raisins and 1oz of the almonds and mix well.

3. Lift the bread out of the milk and squeeze gently to remove some of the liquid. Reserve the milk and add the bread to the slow cooker. Cover and cook for 2 hours.

4. Preheat the oven to 350°F (180°C). Whisk the eggs into the remaining milk and season. Pour over the lamb mixture and sprinkle with the remaining almonds. Transfer the ovenproof part of the slow cooker to the oven and cook for 30 minutes or until the top has set and is golden.

TIP: This is South Africa's answer to shepherd's pie. Sweet and spicy minced lamb is hidden under a golden topping, scattered with flaked almonds. Serve hot with a green salad.

Greek meatballs with egg-lemon sauce

SERVES 4

1. Place 1 cup of stock in a slow cooker on high. Cover and heat.

2. Combine lamb, onion, 1 egg yolk, mint, oregano and parsley in a large bowl. Season with salt and pepper and add remaining stock. Roll tablespoon quantities into balls, then roll lightly in rice.

3. Transfer meatballs into slow cooker. Cover, turn to low and cook for 6 hours.

4. In a medium-sized bowl beat remaining egg yolks, slowly adding lemon juice until combined. Slowly add most of the hot stock from slow cooker, beating constantly until well combined and mixture thickens. Stir over low heat in a small saucepan if necessary. Serve the sauce drizzled over the meatballs.

1½ cups beef stock
17½oz (500g) lean lamb mince
1 small onion, chopped
5 egg yolks
1 teaspoon chopped fresh mint
1 teaspoon chopped fresh oregano
1 tablespoon chopped fresh parsley
salt and freshly ground black pepper
2 tablespoons rice
juice of 1 lemon

Lamb shanks with broad beans, olives & risoni

SERVES 4–6

1. Heat the oil in a large saucepan, add the garlic, lamb shanks and onion and cook for 5 minutes or until the shanks are lightly browned.

2. Transfer to a slow cooker set on low. Add the beef stock, oregano sprigs, tomato paste and water. Cook for 8 hours.

3. Remove the shanks, slice the meat off the bone and set aside.

4. Turn slow cooker onto high and add the risoni and cook for a further 45 minutes. Add the beans, olives, meat, oregano, salt and pepper, cook for 30 minutes more and serve.

TIP: If broad beans are large, peel off outer skin.

2 tablespoons olive oil
2 cloves garlic, crushed
4 lamb shanks
1 onion, chopped
2 cups beef stock
4 sprigs fresh oregano
2 tablespoons tomato paste
2 cups water
1 cup risoni
1 cup broad beans
½ cup black olives
2 teaspoons chopped fresh oregano
salt and freshly ground black pepper

Lamb & spinach curry

SERVES 4

2 tablespoons vegetable oil
2 onions, chopped
2 cloves garlic, chopped
¾in (2cm) piece fresh root ginger,
    finely chopped
1 cinnamon stick
¼ teaspoon ground cloves
3 cardamom pods
26½oz (750g) diced lamb
1 tablespoon ground cumin
1 tablespoon ground coriander
⅓ cup natural yoghurt
2 tablespoons tomato paste
¾ cup beef stock
salt and freshly ground black pepper
3½oz (100g) baby spinach, chopped
2 tablespoons flaked almonds,
    toasted

1. Heat the oil in a large heavy-based saucepan. Add onions, garlic, ginger, cinnamon, cloves and cardamom and cook for 5 minutes.

2. Add the lamb and cook for 5 minutes, turning, until it begins to brown.

3. Transfer to a slow cooker set on high. Mix in the cumin and coriander, then add the yoghurt 1 tablespoon at a time, stirring well each time.

4. Mix together the tomato paste and the stock and add to the lamb. Season to taste. Reduce the heat to low, cover and cook for 7 hours.

5. Stir in the spinach, cover and simmer for another 15 minutes or until the mixture has reduced slightly. Remove the cinnamon stick and the cardamom pods and mix in the almonds. Serve with rice.

TIP: There's plenty of flavour but no chilli in this dish, so it'll be a hit even with those who don't like hot curries. You can serve it with pilau or all-purpose rice.

Minced lamb & aubergine casserole

SERVES 4

1 tablespoon olive oil
1 small aubergine (eggplant), sliced
9oz (250g) lean lamb mince
3 large ripe tomatoes, peeled, sliced
salt and freshly ground black pepper
6 fresh basil leaves, finely shredded
4oz (125g) Swiss cheese, grated

1. Heat oil in a large frying pan over medium heat. Add aubergine and cook until golden brown. Drain on sheets of absorbent paper.

2. Add lamb and cook for 3–4 minutes or until browned. Drain off any excess fat.

3. In a small casserole dish that fits into your slow cooker, arrange a layer of aubergine slices, a layer of minced lamb and a layer of sliced tomato, sprinkled with salt and pepper and half of the basil. Cover with grated cheese. Repeat layers until casserole dish is filled, ending with a cheese layer.

4. Place casserole in a slow cooker and cook on high for approximately 2 hours. If preferred, casserole may be placed under griller for a minute or two to brown cheese topping. Serve with a large leafy green salad.

Slow-simmered lamb shanks with couscous

SERVES 4

1. Heat a large frying pan over a high heat and add lamb and cook until browned. Transfer to a slow cooker set on high.
2. Add the tomatoes, wine, bay leaf, thyme and cinnamon stick. Cover and cook for 3 hours.
3. Add the pumpkin, courgettes, apricots and prunes and cook for a further 2 hours on a low setting or until the vegetables are soft and the lamb starts to come away from the bone.
4. Meanwhile, put the couscous in a large bowl, cover with boiling water and allow to stand for 10 minutes or until all the liquid is absorbed.
5. Serve the lamb shanks on top of the couscous, garnished with the flaked almonds.

TIP: The term Frenched refers to the cutting and scraping of all meat, fat and gristle from the bone, leaving the meaty part virtually fat-free.

4 lamb shanks, French cut
2 cups canned chopped tomatoes
1 cup dry red wine
1 bay leaf
6 sprigs fresh thyme
1 cinnamon stick
7oz (200g) butternut pumpkin,
* chopped*
2 courgettes (zucchini), chopped
8 dried apricots
8 dried prunes
1 cup couscous
2 cups boiling water
2 tablespoons flaked almonds,
* toasted*

Lamb casserole with couscous & gremolata

SERVES 4

1. Season the flour with salt and pepper and spread it on a large plate. Toss the lamb in the seasoned flour until coated. Heat the oil in a large frying pan, add lamb and cook over medium heat for 2–3 minutes each side, until browned. Transfer the browned meat to a slow cooker set on low, using a slotted spoon.

2. Add the bell peppers and the tomatoes to the slow cooker and cook for 10 hours. Meanwhile, mix all the gremolata ingredients together.

3. Prepare the couscous according to the packet instructions, then fluff it up with a fork. Heat the oil in a small frying pan and cook the onion over a medium heat for 10 minutes until golden brown. Add to the couscous and mix well. Sprinkle the gremolata over the lamb casserole and serve with the couscous.

TIP: Gremolata is a mixture of finely cut parsley, garlic and lemon zest. Adding this to the casserole just before serving adds a fresh new dimension of flavour.

2 tablespoons all-purpose (plain) flour
salt and freshly ground black pepper
26½oz (750g) diced lamb, trimmed of excess fat
2–3 tablespoons extra virgin olive oil
1 yellow bell pepper (capsicum), chopped
1 green bell pepper (capsicum), chopped
2 cups canned chopped tomatoes

GREMOLATA
1 clove garlic, finely chopped
3 tablespoons finely chopped fresh parsley
grated rind of 1 lemon

COUSCOUS
2 cups couscous
1 tablespoon extra virgin olive oil
1 large onion, sliced

Indian meatballs in tomato sauce

SERVES 4

17½oz (500g) lean lamb mince
½ cup natural yoghurt
1in (5cm) piece fresh ginger, grated
1 green chilli, deseeded, finely
   chopped
¼ cup chopped fresh cilantro
   (coriander)
2 teaspoons ground cumin
2 teaspoons ground coriander
salt and freshly ground black pepper
2 tablespoons olive oil
1 onion, chopped
2 cloves garlic, chopped
½ teaspoon ground turmeric
1 teaspoon garam masala
6fl oz (170ml) water
14oz (400g) canned chopped
   tomatoes

1. Combine the lamb, 1 tablespoon of yoghurt, ginger, chilli, 2 tablespoons of chopped cilantro, cumin and ground coriander in a large bowl and season with salt and pepper. Shape the mixture into 16 balls.
2. Heat 1 tablespoon of oil in a large saucepan, add meatballs and cook for 10 minutes, turning until browned (you may have to cook them in batches). Drain on absorbent paper and set aside.
3. In a slow cooker on a high setting add the remaining olive oil, onion and garlic and stir. Mix the turmeric and garam masala with 1 tablespoon of the water, then add to onion and garlic. Add remaining yoghurt, 1 tablespoon at a time, stirring well each time.
4. Add the tomatoes, meatballs and remaining water to the mixture and bring to temperature. Cook for 5 hours, stirring occasionally. Sprinkle over the rest of the cilantro to garnish and serve on a bed of rice.

Tarragon lamb

SERVES 4

2oz (60g) butter
36oz (1kg) leg of lamb
15fl oz (450ml) chicken stock
⅔ cup dry white wine
1 bunch fresh tarragon
salt and freshly ground black pepper
1½ tablespoons cornflour
1 tablespoon water
2 tablespoons pouring cream

1. Melt 1½oz (40g) of the butter in a large heavy-based frying pan over medium heat. Add the lamb and cook for 3 minutes or until browned.

2. Transfer to a slow cooker on a low setting and add the remaining butter, stock and wine. Cover and cook for 10 hours.

3. Remove the meat and keep warm. Add the tarragon and seasoning to the cooker, turn to high and reduce the liquid by half. Thicken with the cornflour mixed with the water to form a paste, then add the cream.

4. Taste and adjust the seasoning, then remove the tarragon. Slice the lamb and serve with the reduced sauce and roasted vegetables.

Lamb shanks with root vegetables

SERVES 4

1. Heat 1 tablespoon of the oil in a large heavy-based saucepan, add the root vegetables and cook until brown. Set aside on a plate. Add the extra oil to the pan and brown the garlic and lamb for a few minutes.
2. Transfer the lamb and garlic to a slow cooker set on high and add the stock, water, red wine, tomato paste, rosemary, bouquet garni, pepper and salt. Cook for 30 minutes, then reduce the heat to low and cook for a further 7 hours.
3. Add the vegetables to the slow cooker and continue to cook for another hour, until everything is cooked. Before serving, remove the bouquet garni and check the seasoning.

2 tablespoons olive oil
2 parsnips, cut into large chunks
1 medium sweet potato, cut into
   large chunks
6 pickling onions
2 cloves garlic, crushed
4 lamb shanks
¾ cup beef stock
¼ cup water
½ cup dry red wine
1 tablespoon tomato paste
1 sprig rosemary
1 bouquet garni
salt and freshly ground black pepper

beef

Beef carbonade

SERVES 4

2 tablespoons vegetable oil
36oz (1kg) gravy beef, cut into ¾in
   (2cm) cubes
1 large onion, thinly sliced
1 tablespoon all-purpose (plain) flour
2 tablespoons brown sugar
1½ cups stout
2 cups beef stock
1 tablespoon tomato paste
1 bouquet garni
salt and freshly ground black pepper
chopped fresh parsley to garnish

1. Heat the oil in a large frying pan over medium heat. Add one-third of the beef and cook until browned. Remove from the pan while you cook the remaining batches, adding more oil if necessary. Set the beef aside.

2. Lower the heat, add the onion and cook for 5 minutes, stirring. Sprinkle in the flour and sugar and stir for 1–2 minutes, then add ½ cup of the stout and swirl to collect all of the flavour from the pan. Pour into a slow cooker set on low. Add the remaining stout, stock, sautéed beef, tomato paste and bouquet garni. Season and stir well, then cover.

3. Cook for 10 hours. Stir 2–3 times during cooking, adding a little water if necessary. Discard the bouquet garni and season again if necessary.

Osso bucco

SERVES 4

2 tablespoons olive oil
36oz (1kg) veal osso buco
1–2 tablespoons all-purpose (plain)
  flour
1 clove garlic, crushed
1 onion, finely chopped
1 carrot, finely diced
2 sticks celery, finely diced
½ cup dry white wine
4 Roma tomatoes, peeled, chopped
⅔ cup beef stock
2 tablespoons tomato paste
1 tablespoon chopped fresh basil
1 tablespoon chopped fresh parsley
salt and freshly ground black pepper

1. Heat oil in a large frying pan.

2. Coat osso buco with flour and cook in pan for 3 minutes each side. Remove from the pan and set aside.

3. Add the garlic, onion, carrot and celery to the pan and cook for 5 minutes. Add wine and cook until evaporated.

4. Add the tomatoes, stock and tomato paste to a slow cooker set on low. Add the veal, vegetables and herbs, then season. Cover and simmer for 6½ hours until the meat starts to come away from the bone. Serve with crusty bread.

Mexican-style beef

SERVES 4

1. Place the beef between sheets of non-stick baking paper and flatten. Heat a large frying pan over medium heat. Add bacon and cook for 3 minutes, draining off any excess fat. Remove from the heat and mix with the parsley, marjoram and breadcrumbs.
2. Combine the flour, salt and pepper in a shallow dish. Divide the bacon mixture between slices of the beef, then roll up each slice from the short end, turn it in the seasoned flour and secure it with a toothpick.
3. Heat the oil in a large frying pan over medium heat, add the beef and cook for 2 minutes, turning, until browned. Remove from pan and place in a slow cooker set on low. Add the chilli powder, onion, garlic and bell pepper. Gently pour over the stock. Cover the dish then cook for 6 hours. Add the kidney beans and cook for another 3 hours. Remove the cocktail sticks to serve.

4 thin-cut beef sirloin steaks
4 strips rindless bacon, finely
  chopped
1 tablespoon chopped fresh parsley
½ teaspoon dried marjoram
1 cup fresh breadcrumbs
½ cup all-purpose (plain) flour
salt and freshly ground black pepper
toothpicks
1 tablespoon olive oil
1 teaspoon chilli powder
1 onion, diced
2 cloves garlic, crushed
1 red bell pepper (capsicum), diced
1 cup beef stock
2 cups canned red kidney beans,
  rinsed, drained

Drunken beef

1. In a slow cooker set on high, cook the vegetables in the beer and 2 tablespoons of oil for 10 minutes. Add the meat on top of the vegetables and spoon over the tomato paste. Add the seasoning and herbs. Cook for 1 hour on high then reduce the heat to a low setting.

2. Add the remaining oil and the flour. Stir to combine all ingredients and cook on a low setting for 8 hours.

3. Remove the bay leaf, taste and adjust the seasoning. Serve with toast, if desired.

2 onions, diced
2 carrots, sliced
6 button mushrooms, sliced
⅔ cup beer
¼ cup olive oil
15oz (450g) gravy beef, diced
2 tablespoons tomato paste
salt and freshly ground black pepper
1 teaspoon fresh thyme
1 bay leaf
1 tablespoon all-purpose (plain) flour

Mediterranean beef & olive casserole

SERVES 6

2lb 13oz (1.3kg) lean gravy beef, cut
  into 1in (5cm) pieces
2 tablespoons olive oil
24 pitted black olives, plus 12 to
  garnish
4 tomatoes, quartered, deseeded
salt and freshly ground black pepper
chopped fresh parsley to garnish
grated rind of 1 lemon to garnish

MARINADE
juice of ½ lemon
2 medium onions, chopped
2 cloves garlic, crushed
3 bay leaves
3 sprigs fresh thyme
½ teaspoon fresh oregano
2 tablespoons chopped fresh parsley
1 small bulb fennel, chopped
2 carrots, sliced
8 whole black peppercorns
2 tablespoons olive oil
3 cups dry white wine

1. Combine marinade ingredients, then add the meat and coat. Cover and refrigerate for 2 hours.

2. Remove the meat, reserving the marinade. Heat 1 tablespoon of the oil in a large frying pan over medium heat. Add half the meat and cook for 6 minutes, turning once. Put prepared meat into a slow cooker set on high, then fry the remaining meat and add to slow cooker as well. Stir in the marinade and 24 olives. Cover and cook for 1 hour.

3. Press the meat down with the back of a wooden spoon and top with the tomatoes. Season lightly and drizzle over the remaining oil. Cover the dish again and cook for 5 hours.

4. Adjust seasoning, then sprinkle over the parsley, lemon rind and remaining olives to serve.

Beef braised in red wine

SERVES 4

¼ cup olive oil
24oz (700g) gravy beef, trimmed of
    fat, cut into 2⅓in (6cm) chunks
6 French shallots, finely chopped
2 cloves garlic, crushed
2 sticks celery, sliced
7oz (200g) button mushrooms, sliced
½ teaspoon ground allspice
1½ cups full-bodied red wine
1 cup tomato purée
2 sprigs fresh thyme
salt and freshly ground black pepper

1. Heat the oil in a large saucepan and cook the meat over high heat, stirring, for 5 minutes until browned. Remove from pan, then add the shallots, garlic and celery. Cook, stirring, for 4 minutes until browned. Add the mushrooms and cook for 1 minute or until softened.

2. In a slow cooker set on high add the allspice, wine and tomato purée, then all of the fried ingredients. Add 1 sprig of thyme and the seasoning. Cover and cook for 4 hours.

3. Season again if necessary, then serve garnished with the remaining thyme and mashed potato.

Farmer's casserole

SERVES 4

1. Place the meat and the vegetables in a slow cooker set on a high setting. Stir in the stock and season well. Cover and cook for 3½ hours.

2. Meanwhile, make the dumplings by combining all the dry ingredients in a bowl. Using your fingertips, rub in the butter and water to form a soft dough.

3. Preheat the oven to 350°F (180°C).

4. Shape the dough into 12 equal dumplings. Stir the butter beans and peas into the casserole, taste and adjust the seasoning.

5. Arrange the dumplings over the top and put the uncovered dish in the oven for 30 minutes or until the dumplings are golden.

TIP: This recipe requires you to finish the dumplings in the oven so you will need to use a slow cooker with a cooking dish that can be removed from the electrical component and safely put into the oven.

15oz (450g) gravy beef, trimmed of fat, cut into 1in (25mm) cubes
2 carrots, diced
2 leeks, sliced
1 onion, diced
1 cup beef stock
salt and freshly ground black pepper
14oz (400g) canned butter beans, rinsed, drained
1¾oz (50g) frozen peas

CHEESE DUMPLINGS
3½oz (100g) self-rising (self-raising) flour
1 teaspoon finely chopped fresh parsley
1¾oz (50g) Cheddar cheese, grated
1¾oz (50g) butter, cut into small cubes
2 tablespoons water

Oxtail with black olives

1. Heat a medium non-stick frying pan over high heat. Add oxtail and cook for 2 minutes or until browned.

2. Place oxtail in a slow cooker, add wine and brandy, then cover and cook on high for 30 minutes to bring oxtail to temperature.

3. Add stock, rosemary, orange rind and garlic. Season with salt and freshly ground pepper. Cover and cook for 8 hours on low.

4. Add the olives and cook for a further hour. You may want to reduce the sauce further by straining it into a small saucepan and rapidly boiling it for 5 minutes or until sauce has thickened. Serve on a bed of steamed rice.

TIP: Ask your butcher to cut the oxtail into joints.

2 small or 1 large oxtail, trimmed of fat
¼ cup dry white wine
⅓ cup brandy
1½ cups hot beef stock
3 sprigs fresh rosemary
grated rind of 1 orange
2 cloves garlic, crushed
salt and freshly ground black pepper
1 cup pitted black olives

French onion stew

SERVES 6

3lb 5oz (1.5kg) lean stewing beef,
    trimmed, cut into large cubes
2 tablespoons tapioca
1¾ cup beef stock
3½oz (100g) mushrooms, sliced
2oz (60g) butter
6 medium onions, thinly sliced
pinch salt
¼ cup double cream
fresh thyme leaves to garnish

1. Combine beef, tapioca, stock and mushrooms in a slow cooker, cover and cook on high for 4 hours.

2. Meanwhile, melt butter in a large heavy-based frying pan over low heat. Add onion and cook, stirring, for 45 minutes or until caramelised and dark brown in colour. Add the caramelised onions to the slow cooker and stir to combine. Continue to cook all ingredients together for remaining time.

3. Just before serving stir through cream. Serve the stew on a bed of rice, garnished with fresh thyme.

Mediterranean beef stew

SERVES 6

2 tablespoons oil
36oz (1kg) lean stewing beef,
*   trimmed, cut into large cubes*
2 onions, sliced
2 cloves garlic, chopped
1 aubergine (eggplant), diced
1 cup beef stock
14oz (400g) canned whole peeled
*   tomatoes, chopped*
¼ cup tapioca
1 teaspoon ground cinnamon
1 bay leaf
2 teaspoons salt
freshly ground black pepper
14oz (400g) canned garbanzo beans
*   (chickpeas), rinsed, drained*
fresh oregano leaves to garnish

1.   Heat the oil in a large frying pan over a medium heat. Add meat and cook for 5 minutes, turning occasionally. Add the onions and garlic and cook for a further 5 minutes, stirring constantly. Drain off any excess fats. Place the beef mixture and aubergine in a slow cooker.

2.   Combine stock with juice from canned tomatoes, tapioca, cinnamon, bay leaf, salt and pepper and pour into slow cooker; stir well. Cover and cook on low setting for 8 hours.

3.   Approximately 30 minutes before serving turn to high, stir in garbanzo beans and tomatoes and cook for the remaining time. Serve garnished with fresh oregano leaves.

Beef with artichokes, olives & oregano

SERVES 4

1. In a large heavy-based frying pan heat 1 tablespoon of olive oil, add meat and sear quickly on all sides. Take out and set aside.

2. Heat extra olive oil, add garlic and scallions, and cook for 3 minutes. Take off the heat then add a splash of white wine to collect all of the flavours from the pan.

3. Pour into a slow cooker set on low, add the remaining white wine, then add beef stock, tomato paste, oregano and salt and pepper. Stir to combine, return meat to dish, add artichokes, cover and cook for 8 hours.

4. Add olives in the last 20 minutes of cooking time.

5. Slice the meat and arrange with vegetables; pour the sauce over meat and vegetables to serve.

TIP: To trim artichokes, remove the outer leaves and stems. Place in a bowl of water with lemon juice. This stops the artichokes from going brown.

2 tablespoons olive oil
26½oz (750g) Scotch fillet
1 clove garlic, crushed
1 bunch scallions (spring onions), trimmed, halved
½ cup dry white wine
1 cup beef stock
1 tablespoon tomato paste
2 teaspoons chopped fresh oregano
salt and freshly ground black pepper
2 globe artichokes, trimmed and cut into quarters
⅓ cup black olives

vegetables

Argentinean bean & vegetable stew

SERVES 4

1 tablespoon olive oil
1 onion, finely diced
2 cloves garlic, crushed
1 red bell pepper (capsicum), diced
1 jalapeño chilli, deseeded and diced
1 teaspoon sweet paprika
14oz (400g) canned diced tomatoes
2 cups vegetable stock
9oz (250g) baby potatoes, cut into
  quarters
10½oz (300g) sweet potato, diced
1 carrot, sliced
1 cup fresh peas
14oz (400g) canned cannellini
  beans, rinsed, drained
3 cups shredded savoy cabbage
2 tablespoons freshly chopped
  cilantro (coriander)
salt and freshly ground black pepper

1. Heat oil in a large frying pan over medium heat. Cook onion, garlic, bell pepper and chilli until soft. Add sweet paprika and cook until aromatic.

2. Transfer contents of the frying pan into a slow cooker set on high and add tomatoes and vegetable stock. Stir to combine, then add potato, sweet potato and carrot. Bring to the boil. Reduce heat to low. Cover and simmer for 1½ hours until vegetables are tender.

3. Add peas, beans, cabbage and cilantro and season with salt and pepper. Simmer for a further 30 minutes or until cabbage is cooked.

4. Serve with crusty bread.

Mushroom & barley 'risotto'

SERVES 4

1 tablespoon olive oil
1 onion, diced
9oz (250g) button mushrooms,
    coarsely chopped
3 large Portobello mushrooms, sliced
¼ cup chopped fresh parsley
1 tablespoon chopped fresh thyme
2 cloves garlic, crushed
¾ cup pearl barley
4 cups vegetable stock
2 tablespoons tomato paste
salt and freshly ground black pepper
¼ cup grated Parmesan cheese

1. Heat oil in a large heavy-based saucepan over medium heat. Add onion and sauté for 4 minutes. Add all mushrooms and sauté until golden brown, about 15 minutes. Add the parsley, thyme, garlic and barley and stir for 1 minute.

2. Transfer to a slow cooker set on high, add 4 cups of stock, cover and cook until liquid is almost absorbed and barley is almost tender, about 3 hours.

3. Stir in tomato paste, check for seasoning and cook for a further hour. Until barley is tender and mixture is creamy.

4. Stir in cheese and season again if necessary.

Rich bean & vegetable stew

SERVES 4

1. Cover the porcini mushrooms with 600mL of boiling water, then soak for 20 minutes. Meanwhile, heat the oil in a large saucepan, then add the fresh mushrooms, carrots, potato and green beans and fry gently for 3 minutes.
2. Transfer to a slow cooker set on a high heat setting and add the thyme, sage and garlic, the porcini with their soaking liquid, and the red wine, stock and seasoning. Cook for 45 minutes.
3. Stir in the broad beans, cover and cook for a further 30 minutes. Add the cannellini and flageolet beans to the mixture, then simmer for 15 minutes to heat through.

TIP: This satisfying winter dish is perfect eaten with a hunk of crusty bread to mop up the rich red wine sauce.

4oz (125g) dried porcini mushrooms
¼ cup olive oil
9oz (250g) field mushrooms, chopped
2 carrots, finely diced
1 large potato, diced
9oz (250g) fine green beans, chopped
2 teaspoons dried thyme
2 teaspoons dried sage
2 cloves garlic, crushed
10½fl oz (300ml) dry red wine
2¼ cups vegetable stock
salt and freshly ground black pepper
9oz (250g) frozen broad beans
10oz (310g) canned cannellini beans,rinsed, drained
9oz (250g) canned flageolet beans, rinsed, drained

Kidney beans in plum sauce

SERVES 4

1. Rinse kidney beans well in a strainer under running water. Add the beans and water to a slow cooker set on high. Cook for 2½ hours.

2. Meanwhile, place the basil, cilantro, parsley, cayenne pepper, salt and garlic in a food processor and blend to a paste. Add the jam and vinegar and pulse to combine.

3. After 2½ hours add the paste to the beans and stir gently to coat the beans with the dressing. Turn slow cooker onto low and cook for 1 more hour to allow flavours to penetrate. Garnish with cilantro leaves. Can be served warm or at room temperature.

7oz (200g) dried red kidney beans
2½ cups water
1 tablespoon chopped fresh basil
1 tablespoon chopped fresh cilantro (coriander), plus extra leaves to garnish
1 tablespoon chopped fresh parsley
¼ teaspoon cayenne pepper
salt to taste
1 small clove garlic
⅓ cup plum jam
2 teaspoons red wine vinegar

Okra & bean stew

SERVES 4

2 x 15oz (440g) canned tomatoes
9oz (250g) small okra
2 aubergines (eggplants), chopped
2 onions, chopped
2 cloves garlic, crushed
1 fresh red chilli, deseeded and
    chopped
2 teaspoons olive oil
15oz (440g) canned red kidney
    beans, rinsed, drained
½ cup dry red wine
1 teaspoon brown sugar
¼ cup chopped fresh basil
salt and freshly ground black pepper

1. Add tomatoes, okra, aubergine, onion, garlic, chilli and olive oil to a slow cooker set on high and cook for 30 minutes.

2. Add beans, wine and sugar and cook for a further 2½ hours.

3. Just before serving stir in basil, salt and pepper to taste.

Spiced pumpkin tagine

SERVES 6

1 tablespoon olive oil
1 onion, chopped
1 teaspoon ground coriander
1 teaspoon ground cumin
1 teaspoon allspice
1 green chilli, sliced
14oz (400g) canned chopped
   tomatoes
2 x 14oz (400g) canned garbanzo
   beans (chickpeas), rinsed, drained
14oz (400g) pumpkin, diced
2 cups reduced-salt vegetable stock
⅓ cup couscous
½ cup natural yoghurt
1 tablespoon chopped fresh parsley
   to garnish
1 tablespoon chopped fresh mint to
   garnish

1. Heat the oil in a large frying pan. Add the onion and cook over a medium heat for 5 minutes or until the onion softens. Add the spices and chilli and cook for 2 minutes or until fragrant.
2. Transfer to a slow cooker set on high, then stir in the tomatoes, garbanzo beans, pumpkin and stock and cook for 2 hours.
3. Add the couscous, stir and cover, then turn the cooker off. Let sit for 15 minutes until the couscous is soft.
4. Serve topped with a dollop of yoghurt. Sprinkle with parsley and mint.

Slow vegetable misto

1. Place all vegetables except tomatoes and potatoes in a slow cooker set on low.

2. Combine tomatoes, butter, tapioca, sugar, salt and pepper and lemon rind. Pour over vegetables and stir well. Cover and cook on low for 3 hours or until vegetables are just tender.

3. Add the potatoes and cook for a further 3 hours. Adjust seasoning.

4. Serve topped with flat-leaf parsley and accompanied by fresh crusty bread.

5 sticks celery, cut into 1in (25mm) pieces

12 baby carrots, cut in half lengthwise

2 medium onions, thinly sliced

7oz (200g) fresh green beans

2 green bell peppers (capsicums), cubed

8 baby potatoes

14oz (400g) canned chopped tomatoes

2½oz (80g) butter

2 tablespoons tapioca

pinch sugar

2 teaspoons salt

¼ teaspoon white pepper

1 tablespoon finely grated lemon rind

chopped fresh parsley to garnish

Moroccan potato & lemon casserole

SERVES 4

1. Heat the oil in a frying pan. Add the onions, garlic, chillies, cumin and coriander, then gently fry for 2 minutes to release their flavours.

2. Stir in the potatoes, lemon rind and lemon juice to taste. Transfer to slow cooker on high and add the stock and seasoning. Cover and cook for 3½ hours or until the vegetables are tender and the liquid has reduced slightly.

3. Transfer to plates and top each serving with a spoonful of sour cream. Sprinkle over freshly chopped parsley to garnish.

¼ cup olive oil

2 onions, sliced

3 cloves garlic, chopped

2 red chillies, finely chopped

1 teaspoon ground cumin

1 teaspoon ground coriander

1lb 15oz (900g) kipfler potatoes, cut into ⅛in (5mm) slices

grated rind and juice of 1 lemon

3 cups vegetable stock

salt and freshly ground black pepper

⅓ cup sour cream

¼ cup chopped fresh parsley to garnish

Index

Minced lamb & aubergine
   casserole 136
Moroccan potato
   & lemon casserole 189
Moroccan-style chicken wings 96
Mushroom & barley 'risotto' 176
Okra & bean stew 182
Osso bucco 152
Oxtail with black olives 165
Porcini mushroom soup 34
Pork cutlets with quince 109
Portuguese jugged chicken 90
Portuguese pork with cumin 122
Portuguese potato
   & bean soup 32
Rich bean & vegetable stew 179
Roasted tomato, red pepper
   & bread soup 53
Roma tomato, lentil
   & basil soup 39
Savoury pumpkin soup 47
Seafood casserole 56
Shellfish stew 66
Sienese bean soup 42
Slow chicken with ricotta,
   arugula & red peppers 93
Slow fish stew on
   rosemary mash 63
Slow vegetable misto 187

Slow-simmered lamb shanks
   with couscous 139
Slowfood paella 77
Sour shrimp curry 71
Spanish chicken with chorizo 80
Spanish pea soup 40
Spiced pumpkin tagine 184
Swedish pork meatballs 114
Sweet potato
   & rosemary soup 48
Tarragon lamb 144
Tuscan sausage pot 120

Published in 2013 by
New Holland Publishers
London • Sydney • Cape Town • Auckland

Garfield House 86–88 Edgware Road London W2 2EA United Kingdom
Wembley Square First Floor Solan Road Gardens Cape Town 8001 South Africa
1/66 Gibbes Street Chatswood NSW 2067 Australia
218 Lake Road Northcote Auckland New Zealand

www.newhollandpublishers.com

A catalogue record of this book is available at the British Library and the National Library of
Australia.

ISBN: 9781742573823

Publisher: Fiona Schultz
Design: Lorena Susak
Production Director: Olga Dementiev
Printer: Toppan Leefung Printing Ltd (China)

10 9 8 7 6 5 4 3 2 1

Cover & texture: Shutterstock

Follow New Holland Publishers on

Facebook: www.facebook.com/NewHollandPublishers

UK £9.99
US $14.99